Tennis

R U L E S

Tennis
RULES

BARRY NEWCOMBE
The Express

WARD LOCK

A WARD LOCK BOOK

First published in the UK 1997
by Ward Lock
Wellington House, 125 Strand
LONDON WC2R 0BB

A Cassell Imprint

Distributed in the United States
by Sterling Publishing Co., Inc.
387 Park Avenue South, New York,
NY 10016-8810

A British Library Cataloguing-in-Publication
Data block for this book may be obtained from
the British Library

Photographs by Colorsport

ISBN 0–7063–7538–6

Typeset by Business Color Print, Welshpool,
Powys, Wales
Printed and bound in Great Britain by Bath Press

ACKNOWLEDGEMENTS

The author gratefully acknowledges the
assistance of the International Tennis
Federation and of the Lawn Tennis Association
in the preparation of this book.

Cover Michael Stich playing in the 1991
Wimbledon semi-finals against Stefan Edberg.

Frontispiece Andre Agassi, 1992 Wimbledon
Men's Final winner, playing at Wimbledon in
1995.

CONTENTS

Introduction	6
The Dress	8
The Court	12
The Equipment	18
Starting the Game	22
Scoring	36
Doubles	39
The Officials	41
Behaviour on Court	45
Tournaments	49
Rules Clinic	52
Rankings	55
Useful Addresses	60
Index	63

INTRODUCTION

Tennis is a simple game. It can be played with two players, as in singles, or four players, as in doubles. Whether the players are competing in the Wimbledon final or playing just for fun on a public court, the same rules and objectives apply. At the highest professional level, tennis involves probably no more than 1,000 men and women playing the world tournament circuit; but beyond them, there are millions of players worldwide with differing dreams of fulfilment on a tennis court.

Lawn tennis began as an outdoor version of real or royal tennis, a game which might be as much as 1,000 years old. Real tennis is still played today and some dozen courts are located around the country, notably at Hampton Court, England. The outdoor game developed during the nineteenth century through the enthusiasm and foresight of Major Walter Clopton Wingfield, who devised a set of rules in 1874. Major Wingfield's proposals

meant that he was credited with being the founder of the modern game and within three years of his ground-breaking moves, the All England Croquet and Lawn Tennis Club was to stage its first championship, albeit for men only. A championship for women was introduced in 1884.

A set of rules had been established by the Marylebone Cricket Club in 1875. The All England Club made some amendments of its own and those revised rules form the basis of the rules which are in operation today. The club soon moved the championships from nearby courts to Church Road, Wimbledon, where they have been held ever since. 'Wimbledon', as the tournament is universally known, quickly became established as a mecca for all tennis players and fans.

Tennis has been 'open' since 1968 when restrictions on amateurs playing with professionals were lifted. This paved the way for today's vibrant professional tours for men and women, by providing the opportunity to develop a great range of new tournaments, as well as maintaining the traditions and grandeur of the old. Wimbledon, the Australian, French and US Opens together form the 'Grand Slam' circuit. Winning all four tournaments in the same year is a feat achieved by very few players. In 1988, tennis became an Olympic sport for the first time since 1924, which was an indication of its penetration into some 190 countries.

The Wimbledon championships' administrators and the British tennis authorities have ensured that tennis in Britain continues to attract the world's best players year by year. However, at the same time, standards of British players have been in a decline but there is a vigorous drive to revive and lift them into the twenty-first century and beyond. Over £200 million has already been spent on new facilities so that people who want to play tennis can find somewhere to do so more readily than was previously the case. There is a national network of over 40 indoor centres, with more to come. Of the 25,000 tennis clubs in Britain, many have indoor courts.

As many as 6 million men and women play tennis in Britain each year, using some 37,000 courts. Some courts are privately owned, while others are in public hands. It is a fact that public parks are still the most popular venues for the game. But the rules are the same for all, from Wimbledon champion to public park novice. The rules are laid down by the International Tennis Federation, which has its headquarters in London, and these apply to every match.

THE DRESS

Choose shoes and clothing in which you feel comfortable to play tennis. Tennis clothing was once predominantly white – and still is at Wimbledon – but these days almost anything goes on the court. Wearing the very latest styles may make you look like one of the world's top ten players, but you have to work out whether it suits your personal inclination and, indeed, your pocket to try to keep up with the fashions in a rapidly changing market. Your opponent could be put off by garish clothing and some players most definitely object to their opponent wearing sunglasses (especially the reflective kind). Good sense should prevail on either side of the net – what suits you usually suits your opponent as well.

Tennis shoes should be light, comfortable and should allow good ventilation. A great deal of imagination, thought and investment has gone into the manufacture of

In hotter climates, a headband will absorb sweat which otherwise is likely to affect your vision and concentration. You might also like to wear matching wristbands.

today's tennis shoes and the range of styles and price is considerable. Running around a tennis court for an hour or two makes heavy demands on your feet and it is important to reduce pressure points created by your shoes as much as possible. When you try new shoes on, always wear the type of socks in which you intend to play. If you are uncertain which shoes to choose, look at the shoes worn by players of different ages, abilities, weights and pace. It is unlikely that you will be changing your shoes every other month, so make sure you buy the ones that will suit you best. Remember that you could be playing on different surfaces and in a variety of weather conditions.

The range of tennis clothing is vast. Socks have to feel comfortable and to fit properly. You will need either a tennis shirt and shorts or skirt, or a tennis dress and something warm to wear on top, in addition to a tracksuit for warming up. Outdoor conditions

It is important to choose shoes that are comfortable, lightweight and allow good ventilation. They should also be suitable for most weather conditions.

often make a tracksuit a necessity and it can be useful for indoor play as well. Men can use the pocket in their shorts to carry a spare ball. Women can also use the pocket of their shorts or there are skirts that are available with an internal pocket. Alternatively, you could copy some of the top players, who prefer to carry a spare ball in a lightweight holder on their back.

Wristbands and headbands help to combat sweating and these are especially useful in conditions when perspiration is likely to affect vision and concentration. Adopt the habit of including a towel in the bag that you bring on court. It is permissible for the bag to contain any support materials you might need and these can range from a spare racket(s) to extra clothing, plus food and drink.

A peaked cap can help your vision and concentration – some players, like American Jim Courier, would never go on court without one!

Many players like to wear a peaked cap or simply a visor to aid vision and concentration, especially in strong sunlight or changing light conditions. Whether a cap actually helps is a matter of personal choice and of trial and error, but some players would never go on court without one.

Check you have everything you need before you go out on court. If you feel comfortable, this is one less aspect with which to concern yourself. Your hands and feet are going to do a lot of work once play begins, so pay particular attention to comfort in those areas. It is important that you feel fit to play and that you warm up properly. Allow time for the warm-up and do not rush your preparations. Feel confident in yourself and in the equipment you have selected before launching into the game. If you have any doubts about your physical condition or have experienced an injury, always seek professional medical advice first.

THE COURT

● SURFACES

Tennis is played on such a variety of surfaces these days that it is important to be able to adapt to them all.

Grass
As the name 'lawn tennis' implies, the game was originally played on grass and this continues to be the surface used at the Wimbledon championships, which are the game's showpiece. Other tournaments are played on grass throughout the United Kingdom and on a limited basis elsewhere in the world – notably Austria, Holland, Germany and the United States.

A hard and fast grass court usually benefits the serve-and-volley game of the power player, who uses the speed of the court to enhance his or her natural abilities. Inevitably, this leads to short, punishing rallies played out at high speed between tall, lean and strong players. Rackets that have been developed to produce more powerful shots merely serve to make the best grass-court players even more threatening.

Grass courts need more maintenance than any other surface. Wimbledon has been in the business of producing quality grass courts for more than a century and the techniques involved are handed down from one generation of groundsmen to the next. The courts are only allowed a matter of days to settle down once the championships have ended, before the process of preparing them for the following year is begun.

At the start of the Wimbledon championships (or any other grass-court tournament), the grass is green and moist. Players slip and slide about and can even stretch groin muscles as they adjust to the footing and the pace of the ball. By the end of a tournament, when the grass is worn and brown, the court will slow down a little and the balls will bounce a fraction higher than before and not quite so quickly.

Clay

Some players say that grass is only fit for grazing cows. There has always been a small minority of players who will not play on grass and prefer to use a clay court where patience, endurance and strategy offer different kind of rewards from those of the power game on a fast court. It is no surprise that the player who can win with athleticism, pace and strength at Wimbledon finds it less easy to dominate on a slower court. Usually made from red shale, clay courts are used for the French Open in Paris and for other important European championships.

Artificial

Hard, synthetic outdoor courts usually help the stronger player. They are used for both the Australian and the US championships, which used to be staged on grass. The change to artificial surfaces allowed both nations to develop simultaneously new court complexes and spectator facilities.

A great deal of indoor tennis is played on synthetic carpet surfaces. Growth in this area of the game began in the 1970s in the years immediately after tennis had established itself as an open game. The removal of weather conditions takes away one of the critical factors of outdoor play and gives the shotmaker a chance to develop.

Climate has to be taken into consideration when practising or playing tennis, and this also influences what kind of court surface is practically and financially suited to the area. Certainly, tour players will say that as long as they have access to an indoor court for practice, they will be happy. The adjustments necessary for whatever outdoor surface they are to play on require advance planning and making sure that the correct practice facilities are available.

● LAYOUT

The tennis court is rectangular in shape. It measures 23.77 m (78 ft) in length and 10.97 m (36 ft) in width. These measurements apply to a full-size court, which can be used for both singles and doubles play. Running down each of the longer sides of the court are two strips which are known as tramlines and these are each 1.37 m (4 ft 5 in) wide. Tramline areas are only used for doubles. In singles play, a ball which lands in the tramlines is out.

Net

The court is divided across the middle by a net, which is suspended from a cord or a metal cable of no more than 0.8 cm (⅓ in) in diameter. Cable ends must be attached to or should pass over the tops of two posts, which are not more than 15 cm (6 in) square or 15 cm (6 in) in diameter. These posts should not be higher than 2.5 cm (1 in) above the top of the net cord. The centres of the posts must be 0.914 m (3 ft) outside the court on each side and the net must be 0.914 m (3 ft) high at the posts and 0.914 m (3 ft) at the centre of the court.

The net should be made of mesh that is woven closely enough to prevent the ball from passing through. If the same net is used for doubles and singles, 'singles sticks' have to be used when singles are being played. These sticks are not more than 7.5 cm (3 in) square or 7.5 cm (3 in) in diameter and they have to be situated 0.914 m (3 ft) outside the singles court on each side. Usually the net can be adjusted by turning a handle that is fitted on to one of the support posts. The net is stabilized in the middle by a metal cable or a cord, which must be not less than 5 cm (2 in) wide and covered by white tape.

The court is marked out on either side of the net with identically-sized lines, which should be the same colour (usually white). Lines running across each end are known as baselines and those on the side extremities are called the sidelines.

Despite the rain the grass courts at Wimbledon are regarded as the finest in the world.

The exact court dimensions for both singles and doubles.

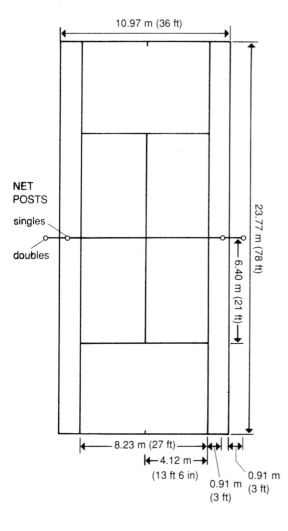

NET POSTS

singles

doubles

10.97 m (36 ft)

23.77 m (78 ft)

6.40 m (21 ft)

8.23 m (27 ft)

4.12 m (13 ft 6 in)

0.91 m (3 ft)

0.91 m (3 ft)

Service court

At a distance of 6.40 m (21 ft) on each side of the net and running parallel to it, are the service lines. The area between the service line and the net is divided exactly in half lengthways by the centre service line. On each baseline, positioned exactly in line with the centre service line, the centre mark (10 cm (4 in) in length and 5 cm (2 in) wide) is drawn. All the other lines, with the exception of the baseline, are no more than 5 cm (2 in) and no less than 2.5 cm (1 in) in width. The baseline should not be more than 10 cm (4 in) wide and remember that all measurements are to the outside of the lines.

Advertisements (or any other material displayed at the back of the court or on the chairs of the linesmen) should not contain white or yellow shades of colour. In fact, any light colour should be used sparingly in case it interferes with the vision of the players.

At club level, the rules recommend that the space behind each baseline

If the same net is to be used for both singles and doubles, 'singles sticks' are put in place whenever the singles game is played.

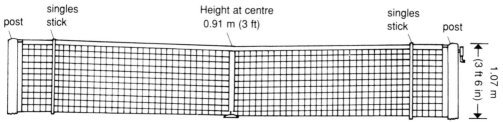

post

singles stick

Height at centre 0.91 m (3 ft)

singles stick

post

1.07 m (3 ft 6 in)

should not be less than 5.5 m (18 ft), and not less than 3.05 m (10 ft) beyond the sideline. For top level competition, the distances increase to 6.4 m (21 ft) and 3.66 m (12 ft).

A net judge sports protective goggles and rests one hand gently on the net so that he will know immediately whether to call a 'let'.

Permanent fixtures

Permanent fixtures are another consideration. These take into account not only the net, posts, cords and supports, but also any stands and fixed or movable seats or chairs positioned around the court. The term is also taken to refer to the occupants of the seats, in addition to court officials, such as the umpire and various line judges, the net cord judge and the ball boys and girls, when they are all in their appointed positions.

THE EQUIPMENT

● TENNIS RACKETS

There is a vast choice of tennis rackets available on the market. All frames were once wooden, but new technology has increased manufacturing possibilities and thus the range available to the would-be purchaser. Today, graphite is the main material used for tennis rackets. Usually, the more expensive the racket, the better the quality is likely to be.

Quite apart from the differences in the material used, there are variations in the shape of the racket head and the width of the frame. The oval frame remains the most popular on the professional circuits but pear shape, teardrop shape and flat-top shapes are among those that are widely used.

Overall length of the frame and handle must not exceed 72.5 cm (29 in). (This rule also comes into effect for non-professional play on 1 January 2000.) The overall width must not exceed 31.75 cm (12.5 in). The strung surface must not exceed 39.37 cm (15.5 in) in overall length and 29.21 cm (11.5 in) in overall width.

When buying a racket, pretend you are shaking hands with it to make sure the grip feels comfortable. Check that the racket handle is neither too small nor too large because, in the long term, either of these situations may lead to strains on the forearm. Similarly, consider the weight of the racket. A heavy racket may tire the arm, but a racket which is too light for the user could affect control of the ball. The sweet spot is another consideration. This is the effective hitting area of the racket; if the ball is hit there it will have maximum impact. If the ball is struck outside the area of the sweet spot, towards the frame, the impact is less.

The whole frame of the racket, including the handle, must be free of objects and devices other than those that limit or prevent wear and tear or vibration or are used to distribute weight. These items must be reasonable in size and placement. Vibration dampeners have to be placed outside the pattern of the crossed strings so that they are out of range of possible contact with the ball.

The hitting surface of the racket has to be flat and consists of a pattern of crossed strings connected to the frame. Stringing patterns must be uniform and should not be less dense in the centre than in any other area. Experience tells a player whether his or her racket is strung to the correct tension, which may vary from player to player. If you break a string during play, you may continue if it is practicable or change the racket. When having a string or strings replaced, make sure the stringer knows your requirements.

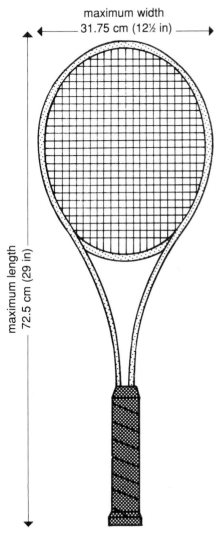

A composite racket with a wide grip and strong shaft is ideal for heavy play.

● TENNIS BALLS

The tennis ball used to be white, but when indoor tournaments began to grow in popularity around the world, a yellow ball was introduced because it was easier to see. Since then, a yellow ball has been adopted almost universally. Wimbledon has been using these balls since 1986.

The ball must be either yellow or white in colour and if it is seamed, these must be without stitches. Pressure inside the ball has to be such that when it is dropped from a height of 2.54 m (100 in) on to a concrete surface, it will bounce between 135 and 147 cm (53–58 in). The ball has to be not more than 6.35 cm (2.5 in) in

When buying a racket, imagine that you are shaking hands with it to check that the grip is comfortable. The same grip is used for receiving service. This photograph shows Virginia Wade at Wimbledon in 1977.

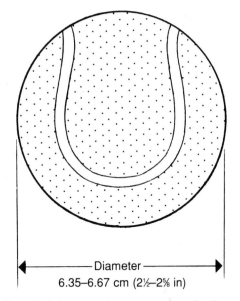

The officially recognized dimensions for the tennis ball

size and less than 6.67 cm (2.625 in) in diameter (a difference of ⅛ in). For those who play at an altitude of more than 1,219 m (4,000 ft), other specifications may apply, so make sure you check with the authorities in advance.

In competitive play, six balls are used. They are changed after seven games and then after every nine games. The balls are changed because their shape and pressure alters under the stress of being hit so frequently. Many tournaments keep supplies of new balls refrigerated to preserve them in perfect condition.

STARTING
THE GAME

● THE WARM-UP

Warming up is an essential part of playing tennis. Some people like to play a few points half an hour or so before they are due to play, but much of the main warm-up can be done in the dressing-room just before the match. Methods vary considerably. The object is to warm up the body and send the blood flowing strongly to the muscles, which are about to be put under stress. Stretching exercises, beginning with the bigger muscle groups and moving through individual muscles are essential. No one should be exhausted by their warm-up. The plan is to left feeling totally ready for competition. It is, of course, just as important to warm down with a similar range of exercises after playing.

All players should have the opportunity to knock up on court just before the match begins. If you are taking part in a recognized tournament with a chair umpire, the countdown to playing the match will be timed and controlled. The umpire will call 'Two minutes', then 'One minute' and finally

Bench press exercises will increase the power of your arms and chest so that you will be able to play rallies for longer periods without tiring.

'Time. Prepare to play', at which point the balls will be sent to the server's end of the court.

If you are injured during the warm-up on court, the rules allow for a 90-second treatment time at the end of the warm-up period. Following this, if you still cannot compete, you waive the match.

Should the match be suspended, for reasons of bad light, ground conditions or the weather, another three-minute warm-up is allowed, if the delay has been between 10–20 minutes. A five-minute warm-up is allowed, if the delay has been more than 20 minutes. No warm-up is allowed for up to a ten-minute delay.

Stretch and develop your side muscles with left and right bends.

The 'cotton picker' is an excellent exercise for the back of the legs. Keeping your knees straight, try to touch your heels and shoes. This will help to prevent cramps in long matches.

Squat press movements will help prevent injuries to knee joints. These are all too frequent in tennis because of the constant bending, stretching and twisting movements.

● STARTING TO PLAY

You are ready to play once you have a racket, balls, an opponent and a court. If you are playing a match, you have to decide whether it will be over the best of three sets or the best of five.
Usually, only men play the best of five-set tennis.

To decide who serves first, a coin is tossed or you could spin a racket. The umpire will toss the coin in a match situation.

The next decision concerns who serves first. Toss a coin or spin a racket. The player who wins the toss chooses whether to serve or to receive. If he/she elects to serve, his/her opponent decides from which end of the court he/she wants to play. Alternatively, the winner of the toss may choose from which end to play and his/her opponent chooses whether to serve or receive. It is generally considered an advantage to serve first. If the match is suspended at this point, with the players at their allotted ends, the original toss stands, but fresh choices may be made on service and end of court when play resumes.

● SERVICE

To start a game, the first service is made from the server's right-hand side of the court. A ball must be struck over the net and into the service court diagonally opposite. The server has to stand between the centre mark and near the sideline. Using his/her non-racket hand, the server puts the ball into the air and strikes it with his/her racket before the ball hits the ground. The serve is complete the moment the racket makes contact with the ball.

It is more usual to use an overhead action to serve, but underarm serves are permissible. You must check with the umpire first and tell your opponent what you intend to do and then stick to your decision. It is not permissible to change from underarm to overhead (or vice versa) randomly throughout the match. A player who can use only one arm may use the racket to project the ball before striking it.

It is regarded as a fault if:

- the ball lands outside the confines of the diagonally opposite service court
- the ball goes into the net
- your foot touches the baseline (footfault)
- you miss the ball when you attempt to serve
- the ball, after it is served, touches a permanent fixture other than the net, strap or band

If the server decides not to strike the ball when it is thrown up and catches it instead, that is not a fault.

If the first serve is a fault, the server is allowed a second serve from the same side of the court. If the second serve is also a fault, the point goes to the opponent and the server moves to the opposite side of the baseline for his/her next service. The server alternates from one side of the centre mark to the other.

Should the server serve from the wrong side, lose the point and then claim a fault, he/she will have to accept that the point stands and the next service should be made from the correct side relating to the score.

The server should not serve until the receiver is ready to play. If the receiver attempts to return the serve, he/she is judged to have been ready to play.

If any part of the foot touches the baseline as the ball comes into contact with the racket, this is regarded as a footfault.

The left foot is pointing towards the net post and the racket is directed towards the service court.

The ball is thrown directly above the player's head.

As the ball goes up, the player takes his racket back.

The player stretches into the air to give extra force to his serve.

Contact is made at the top of the player's reach.

The movement is completed with a follow-through swing.

'Let'

A 'let' applies if:

- the ball touches the net, strap or band before landing in the correct service court
- after touching the net, the ball touches the receiving player or anything he/she is wearing or carrying before hitting the ground
- the server throws up two balls instead of one
- the receiver is not ready
- the ball is broken during play
- there is any uncertainty about the passage of a point

Footfaults

You can be footfaulted even if you do serve the ball accurately. You must not change your position during the service by walking, running or by slight movements of the feet. If either foot touches the baseline in the area between the centre mark and the sideline before the service is complete, that is a fault. Two footfaults in succession mean that the server loses a point.

● WINNING AND LOSING POINTS

The ball is in play from the moment it is struck by the server's racket. If it is a good serve, the receiver tries to return the ball over the net and into the confines of the court. The rally continues until one player hits the ball into the net or out of the court or is unable to make a return, i.e. the ball remains in play until the point is decided. If the receiver makes a doubtful return, but no call is made and the ball remains in play, the server cannot claim the point after the rally has ended.

There are a variety of ways in which points are won and lost. The point is lost if:

- you serve two faults in succession (known as a double fault)
- you allow the ball to bounce twice before returning it over the net
- you do not return the ball over the net after it has been served into the correct service court
- you hit the ball into the net
- your shot hits the ground, or a permanent fixture or any other object, outside the lines of your opponent's court
- you deliberately carry or catch the ball on your racket, or deliberately touch it more than once with your racket
- you (or anything you are wearing or carrying, including your racket), touch the net, posts, singles sticks, cord or metal cable, strap or band, or the ground within your opponent's court at any time while the ball is in play

Jim Courier of the USA in mid-rally during the 1993 Wimbledon Championships. Play is almost continuous from the first service.

- you volley the ball before it has crossed the net
- the ball touches you or something you are wearing or carrying, other than the racket in your hand(s)
- you throw your racket, even if it hits the ball
- you deliberately and materially change the shape of your racket during the playing of a point
- you jump over the net into your opponent's court while the ball is still in play

The shot is regarded good if:

- the ball touches the net, post, singles sticks, cord or metal cable, strap or band in passing over any of the aforementioned and hits the ground within the court
- the ball, whether it is served or returned, hits the ground within the proper court. rebounds or is blown over the net, and the player whose turn it is to strike reaches over the net and plays the ball
- the ball is returned outside the posts or singles sticks, above or below the level of the top of the net, but hits the ground within the proper court, even though it touches the posts or singles sticks
- your racket passes over the net after you have returned the ball, provided the ball had cleared the net before you played it and was properly returned
- you succeed in returning the ball, served or in play, which then strikes another ball lying on the court. Play continues whenever this happens, but if the umpire is uncertain that the right ball is returned, a 'let' is called. You may request that a loose ball or balls lying in your opponent's court be removed, but not while a ball is in play

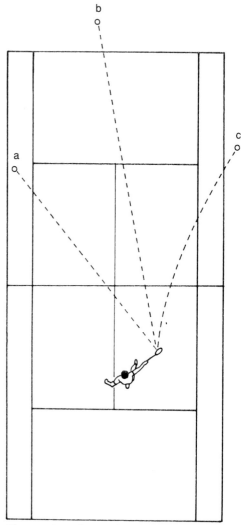

Shots a, b and c would all be classed as out in singles. However, if you were playing doubles shot a would be in.

- the ball, when it is served, touches the receiver or anything he/she is wearing or carrying before the ball hits the ground

Debatable points

In serving, a player occasionally loses the grip on his/her racket and it flies from his/her hand. If the racket hits the net *before* the ball has touched the ground, the server loses the point. Should the racket touch the net *after* the ball has hit the ground outside the lines of the proper court, this is a fault and the server may use his/her second serve.

If you are standing outside the court and catch the ball, you cannot claim the point on the grounds that the ball was going out. Should you volley it and make a bad return, you lose the point; but if the volley is good, the point continues to be played.

If you do anything which hinders your opponent in making a stroke and this is considered deliberate, you lose the point. When this is accidental, the point is replayed.

If the ball or any part of the ball falls on a line of the court in use, it is regarded as 'in'. For a ball to be judged out, it has to be *completely* outside the line.

If the ball in play touches a permanent fixture – apart from the net posts, singles sticks, cord or metal cable, strap or band – *after* it has hit the ground, the player who struck it wins the point; if this is *before* the ball hits the ground, the opponent wins the point. Should a return hit the umpire (or his chair or stand) and even if it is likely that the ball was going into court, the player who hit it loses the point.

● CHANGING ENDS

After the first game, the players change from one side of the net to the other and then reverse their roles. The server becomes the receiver and the receiver serves. They change ends after the odd-numbered games in each set. If a set finishes on an even number of games – 6–4 for example – the change of ends is not made until after the first game of the next set.

If a player serves out of turn, the one who should have served must do so as soon as the mistake is discovered. All the points scored still stand. If a game is finished before the discovery is made, service continues as altered.

Should the players not change ends at the correct time, they must take up the correct position as soon as the discovery is made.

● HINDRANCE

- If a player is hindered into making a bad stroke by something outside his/her control, a 'let' is called. For example, a bird could fly across a player's sight-line as he/she is serving, or land on the court while a rally is in play. In both instances, a 'let' is played

- No 'let' is allowed if the player is hindered by a permanent fixture of the court
- A player who hinders an opponent deliberately loses the point. If the hindrance is involuntary, the point is replayed
- A player may claim a 'let' if a spectator gets in his/her way and prevents him/her from returning the ball. The umpire will allow the 'let' if he/she believes the player was obstructed by circumstances beyond his/her control. In this example, if the player is serving and has had one fault, the 'let' allows two more serves
- If a ball in play hits another ball in the air, a 'let' is called – unless one of the players has caused the other ball to be in the air. In this case the umpire decides whether it is a deliberate act of hindrance
- If an umpire or other court official mistakenly calls 'fault' or 'out' and then corrects him/herself, a 'let' must be called (unless the umpire is certain that neither player was hindered, in which case the corrected call stands)
- If the first ball served is a fault and then rebounds on to the court, interfering with the receiver at the time of the second service, the receiver may claim a 'let' – but not if he/she had an opportunity to remove the ball from the court and failed to do so
- If the ball touches a stationary object on the court, the stroke is good – unless the object was put into the court after the ball was put into play. In this case, a 'let' is called
- If the ball in play strikes an object moving along or above the surface of the court, a 'let' must be called
- If the second serve is good, and it then becomes necessary to call a 'let' (as itemized above) or the umpire is unable to decide the point, the fault is annulled and the whole point is replayed

In this illustration only ball f is out, which demonstrates what a difficult job the line judges have.

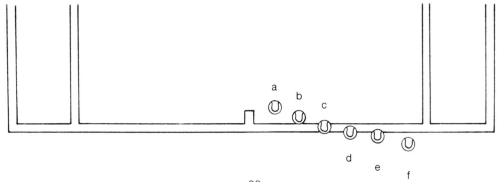

● CONTINUOUS PLAY

Generally, the rule is that play should be continuous from the first serve until the match is over. However, an umpire may suspend or delay play at any time, if he/she considers it necessary and appropriate.

The server must set a reasonable pace and the receiver must not delay in being ready to receive the serve. There should be a maximum of 20 seconds from the moment the ball goes out of play until the start of the next point. When changing ends, a period of up to 90 seconds is allowed. These limits apply to major tournament play and team events recognized by the International Tennis Federation and are also used at other levels of the game. If the umpire feels that the principle of play being continuous is being violated, he/she may give a warning and then disqualify the offending player.

Injury

A player cannot be given additional time to recover his/her breath, strength or physical condition. In the case of accidental injury, one three-minute suspension of play is allowed for treatment. This may begin

Conchita Martinez of Spain experiences a painful cramped muscle during the 1994 Wimbledon Women's Singles Final. Her trainer is allowed on the court for a three-minute suspension of play.

immediately, or may be delayed until the player who has made the request decides that he/she is ready to receive treatment. The suspension of play then begins at the end of an even game, or at the next changeover, when the total time allotted for the changeover becomes four and a half minutes.

In women's tennis, a player who sustains an injury may be allowed a three-minute suspension of play. This time begins when the trainer or doctor arrives on court. If two injuries occur at the same time, the player may have a maximum of two three-minute treatment periods in a row.

In order to be defined as accidental, an injury has to be the result of a visible accident such as a fall or collision, or a sudden sprain or pull. Any display of blood will be judged as an accident. The gradual deterioration of a pre-existing ailment or normal physical condition is not an accidental injury.

During the regular changeover, a player may receive treatment or examination; such treatment should not exceed two consecutive changeovers. The player may not receive hands-on treatment for natural loss of physical condition; injections or oxygen may not be administered on court.

If a player is injured during the warm-up period, he/she is allowed a 90-second treatment period at the end of the warm-up. If the player is then not physically able to compete, the match will not start.

Toilet break

In men's tennis, a player may leave the court once for a toilet break in a three-set match, twice during a five-set match. The break should be taken at a changeover. In women's tennis, a player is entitled to a maximum of two breaks per match and in doubles, each team is entitled to a maximum of two breaks. Women may take a toilet break, not exceeding five minutes, when necessary. If the break is taken at a changeover, an additional 90 seconds is allowed.

Changing clothes

Should a problem develop with clothing, footwear or equipment (except the racket) through circumstances beyond the player's control, making it impossible or undesirable to play on, the umpire may suspend play for the maladjustment to be corrected. Women players are permitted to change their clothes off court, but this may be done only at a changeover and the time allowed is six and a half minutes.

Rest period

After a third set – or a second set when women are playing – either player may take a rest not exceeding ten minutes. If you happen to be playing 15 degrees north or south of the equator, you can claim a 45-minute break.

Boris Becker changes his shirt during a lengthy match in one of the early rounds of Wimbledon 1990.

SCORING

The score of the server is always called before the score of the receiver, except in the tie-break, when the score of the leading player is called first. If the tie-break score is level, it is called 'One-all' and so on.

● GAMES

To win a game, a player must win a minimum of four points. The first point to be won is called '15'. If it is won by the server, the score is '15-love'. A score of no points is referred to as love' rather than 'nil', 'zero' or 'nought' (except in the tie-break, when 'zero' is used). The second point is called '30', and the third point '40'. If the same player wins a fourth point, he/she wins the game. However, if the opponent wins the next point at '15-love', the score goes to '15-all'.

If both players win three points, the score is called 'deuce' (rather than '40-all'). The next point won is called 'advantage' and accompanied by the name of the player who wins it. If the same player wins the next point, he/she wins the game. If the opposing player wins it, the score reverts to 'deuce' and the game continues until one player wins two points in a row from deuce, which decides the game in his/her favour.

A scoring sequence could progress like this: '15-love', '30-love', '40-love', 'game'. This is referred to as winning a service game to love, i.e. without the opponent gaining a point.

A losing sequence for the server could progress like this: '15-love', '30-love', '30-15', '30-all', '30-40', 'game'.

Automatic scoreboards allow spectators who arrive mid-match to assess the situation immediately. In top-level tennis, men's matches consist of five sets, but otherwise it is generally the best of three.

● SETS

The first player to win six games, with a two-game margin over his/her opponent, wins the set. When a set is decided, the score is called by the umpire 'Game and first set [player's name], six games to four', or whatever the score may be. If necessary, the players carry on until the two-game margin is achieved, so it is quite possible for a set to consist of more than six winning games. The alternative is to play a tie-break at six games all.

The tie-break may be used in all sets or omitted in the last one of a three-set or five-set match, when normal scoring applies. Make sure before a match starts that everyone knows which scoring system is in use.

In top level competition, men's matches consist of five sets, but otherwise matches are generally the best of three sets. A player must therefore win either three (in the case of a five-setter) or two (in the case of a three-setter) to win the match. If a player wins the first three or two sets, it is not necessary to play the remaining ones and he/she is said to have won the match in straight sets.

● TIE-BREAK

The tie-break, which has been in use for more than twenty years, uses straightforward numbers for scoring, rather than '15', '30', '40', 'deuce', etc. So '1–0' would be called 'One-zero'. The winner of the tie-break is the player who is the first to score seven points, with a two-point margin over his/her opponent.

Tie-break comes into operation at six games all. The player who is due to serve next, serves for the first point. His/her opponent serves for the second and third points, and play continues with each player serving for two points consecutively until the winner of the tie-break (and thus the set) is decided.

The first serve in the tie-break is from the right-hand court and then each service is delivered alternately from the right and left courts. If someone serves from the wrong court, the error has to be corrected at once; but all points played stand.

Players change ends after six points of the tie-break have been completed and then again after each six-point sequence. At the end of the tie-break, the players change ends once more.

The tie-break counts as one game for the ball-change sequence. But if the balls are due to be changed at the beginning of the tie-break, the change is delayed until the second game of the following set.

DOUBLES

Playing doubles increases the number of players on court to four. Only a few adjustments to the rules are required to accommodate this.

The doubles court is bigger than the singles court, taking in the area covered by the tramlines outside the singles court to produce a total width of 10.97 m (36 ft).

Order of serving in doubles is decided at the start of each set. The pair who serve the first game of each set decide which of them is to serve first and the opponents make the same decision for the second game. In the third game, the partner of the player who served in the first game now serves. The partner of the player who served in the second game serves in the fourth. Order is maintained in all subsequent games in the set.

If a tie-break is played in doubles, the player whose turn it is to serve is the server of the first point. The players then serve in rotation for two points each until the winners of the tie-break (and thus the set) are decided.

For receiving serve in doubles, the order is decided at the start of each set. The player who receives the first service does so in every odd game throughout the set. Opposing players decide who shall receive the first service in all even-numbered games.

If a player serves out of turn, the proper order of serving must be applied as soon as the mistake is discovered. All points scored (and any faults served) still stand. If a game is completed before this is discovered, the order of serving remains as altered.

Should the order of receiving be swapped by accident, it remains unaltered until the end of the game in which the mistake is discovered. The next time the pair receive, the original format must be resumed.

Once the ball is in play in doubles, either player in the pair may play the ball. One player in a pair may play all the shots (if the couple are in agreement!)

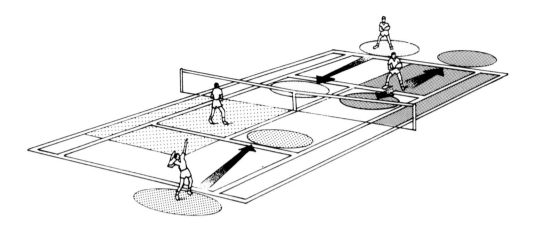

If the server hits his own partner with the service, he incurs a fault. But if the serve hits the receiver's partner before the ball hits the ground, the serving team wins the point.

The partner of the server or receiver may stand anywhere, in or out of the court, as he/she chooses.

If one of a double partnership fails to arrive, the player who is ready to compete is not allowed to play on his/her own against a doubles pair.

Standard doubles positions. The shaded areas show the possible areas of movement for each player. The server can either stay back or come to the net. The server's partner plays in the middle of the service box, ready to intercept balls that go near him. The receiver can either play behind the baseline or move forward to play at the net. The receiver's partner starts out on the service line.

THE OFFICIALS

The higher up the ladder you go in tennis, the more likely you are to have an umpire for your matches. Umpires and teams of line judges seated around the court are obligatory in major tournaments and competitions around the world. When an umpire is in place, his/her decisions are final. But many matches are played without an official in charge and the players then have to choose their own methods of making decisions and resolving any disputes.

● UMPIRES

An umpire has to be totally familiar with all aspects of the rules of tennis and must ensure that the rules are observed by players and other officials on court. He/she may remove, replace or rotate any of the line judges or net umpire if he/she believes that this will improve the officiating. Courtesy, just as much as the rules of the game, dictates that the umpire is able to pronounce the players' names correctly when they meet at the courtside.

Before the knock-up begins, the umpire tosses a coin in the presence of both players – or all four in the case of a doubles match – to decide who is to serve first and who has choice of ends. If play is suspended at this point, the result of the toss stands, but when the match starts, players may choose again.

The umpire keeps the scorecard and announces the score after each point, repeats any calls of the officiating team which have been made in a weak or unclear voice, and confirms any close calls. He/she also has to keep control of the crowd.

The umpire, who must ensure before the match begins that there are sufficient balls available, is responsible for all ball changes and for deciding if a ball is fit for use.

A line judge is kept on the alert throughout Wimbledon 1990.

● LINE JUDGES

A line judge must take up a position on the court that allows the best view of his/her line and should make calls for that line only. He/she should not call 'out' until the ball actually goes out. If the umpire overrules a call, he/she must remain silent.

Line judges should not catch balls or hold towels for players. They must not speak to spectators or applaud players and may not leave the court without the permission of the umpire.

● DIVISION OF DUTIES

The line judges decide the validity of serves, including footfaults, and call when the ball is hit out on the baseline and sidelines. The net-cord judge, as the name implies, is there to signal if a serve hits the net cord.

Line judges' decisions are final on questions of fact, but if the umpire believes that a clear mistake has been made, he/she has the right to change the decision and order a 'let' to be played. If a line judge is unable to give

On a clay court, the umpire may leave his/her chair to make a ball-mark inspection.

The umpire determines if a court is fit for play. If he/she suspends play because the court is unfit or due to adverse weather conditions, he/she must ensure that all officials are ready to resume quickly when conditions improve. Should play be suspended because of darkness, it must be at the end of a set or after an even number of games within a set.

In the event of a dispute, the umpire's decision is usually final although in extreme cases players can appeal for the tournament referee.

a decision, usually because they do not have a clear view, then he/she must indicate this to the umpire straightaway. Should the umpire be unable to make a decision on a question of fact, a 'let' should be played.

An umpire may not overrule one of his line judges for an earlier mistake at the end of a rally. He/she must do so immediately the mistake is made. The umpire can overrule only when he/she considers a call was incorrect beyond all reasonable doubt.

A line judge can change his/her call even after the umpire has called the score, but such a correction must be made immediately he/she realizes the error.

The umpire will not overrule a line judge as the result of a protest or appeal by a player.

● TOURNAMENT REFEREE

If the tournament has a referee, he/she is in charge of all the preparations, organization of the match schedules and officiating. Players can appeal to him/her on questions of tennis law. When a referee is called to a court by the umpire, he/she will ask the umpire to state his/her ruling on the applicable law and should then ask the player for his/her viewpoint. After reviewing the rule the referee then confirms or reverses the original decision. Questions of fact are the responsibility of the on-court officials.

Wimbledon referee, Alan Mills, confers with Michael Stich of Germany.

BEHAVIOUR ON COURT

Proper behaviour on court is one more thing to concentrate on, if you are going to play tennis successfully. If you distract your opponent (or yourself) by your behaviour, you are inviting sanctions. Time-wasting and gamesmanship are considered to be unsporting conduct.

Professional tennis has had a code of conduct since 1976. Penalty points are given for delaying a game, abuse of a racket or verbal abuse. If the behaviour continues, sanctions may include a default, which means that the player is dismissed from the tournament.

Obviously, the code of conduct cannot be operated outside the highest levels of the game for which it was designed, but its principles can be observed no matter where you play.

There are plenty of unwritten rules. For instance, wherever you play, make sure you leave the court as clean and tidy as possible. If you belong to a club, you will be expected to observe club rules. Those same rules should be applied if you are playing on a public court.

If you have entered a tournament, be ready to play whenever you are required. When you are given a court on which to practise, use your allotted time (which is rarely very much) to the limit. You must wear officially recognized tennis clothing. The referee may use his/her discretion in allowing players to wear tracksuits or waterproof clothing in adverse weather conditions, or for medical reasons. Tennis shoes, which have the approval of the host club, must be worn. You must not wear shoes which could, in the opinion of the referee, cause damage to the court surface. A player has to be properly attired and ready for play whenever the match is called. If he/she is not ready within 15 minutes, he/she is liable to be defaulted.

The minute you step on court for a match, you are assumed to be fit to play, even if it hurts whenever you run

or hit the ball. Those are your problems alone.

Any professional player will confirm that tennis is as much a mental as a physical game. You have to sort out your feelings (especially about your weaknesses) and then put in the right amount of work and concentration to help overcome any doubts. Players do not play themselves out of losing situations through good luck alone.

If you are upset by a doubtful line

When a line decision goes against you, you must put it out of your mind for the rest of the match and concentrate on the next point. Here, John McEnroe discusses a ruling during a match against Kevin Curren.

While coaches are a source of support to players, they are only allowed in team competitions and when players change ends at the conclusion of a game. This photograph shows Jennifer Capriati with coach Marty Riessen.

call and feel you must query it with the umpire, do so politely and abide by his/her decision with a good grace. If it goes against you, you must put the decision out of your mind for the rest of the match and concentrate on the point being played. Walking off the court in a temper will lead to a default. In fact, whatever the circumstances, if a player leaves the court during play without the umpire's permission, he/she may be defaulted.

TOURNAMENTS

Tournaments that are recognized in the United Kingdom are sanctioned by the game's governing body – the Lawn Tennis Association. The LTA runs tournaments under the rules laid down by the International Tennis Federation (ITF), plus some additional rules of their own. In other countries, the national association sanctions tournaments, again under the 'umbrella' of the ITF.

Generally, in order to play in a recognized tournament, a player must have a rating under the LTA-registered membership scheme. The exceptions to this are whenever the event is for players aged ten or under, is a handicap event or carries world-ranking points for the Association of Tennis Professionals or the Women's Tennis Association.

Unless it is a team event, most tournaments are organized on a knock-out basis. By signing the entry form, players agree to comply with all the tournament rules and regulations.

When entering the doubles event, both players must submit an entry form. Tournament organizers issue a prospectus with the entry form stating the name, date and location of the tournament, with the full address of the site. The number and type of courts to be used is included; also the manufacturer's brand of balls and whether floodlights may be used. Projected days and times of play are also stated, plus the duration of matches and when and whether the tie-break will be called into operation.

Most tournaments nominate 'seeded' players, which means those players whose record suggests that they will be the strongest players in the tournament. By seeding them, i.e. anticipating where they will finish in the tournament and making the draw in two halves, the organizers ensure that such players cannot meet in the early rounds. The number of seeds to be nominated depends on the overall number of entries:

Up to 15 players	2 seeds
16–23 players	4 seeds
24–31 players	6 seeds
32–47 players	8 seeds
48–63 players	12 seeds
Over 64 players	16 seeds

If the number of entries in singles competitions does not divide exactly by two, 'byes' have to be inserted in the first round only. 'Byes' are given to the seeded players from the top in the order of seeding. If there is still a need for byes after the seeded players have all been given one, they are placed as evenly as possible throughout the draw, Once the seeds and byes are in position in the draw, the remaining players are drawn by lot.

The referee decides on the order of play and which matches take place on which courts. When matches are finished, he/she has to be given the completed scorecards and record the results on his/her master copy. Depending on the size of the tournament, the referee may have a team of assistants to help spread the work load and ensure that there is minimal delay between matches.

In team events, only one court is used, i.e. in the Davis Cup for men and the Federation Cup for women. These are competitions between nations,

Glorious weather conditions prevail for the start of the Australian Open.

rather than individuals. Three days are allocated for matches, with two singles on the first and last days and doubles on the second day. As with all team competitions, the captain may sit at the courtside and advise the players during the changeovers.

● GRAND SLAM CHAMPIONSHIPS

Australian Open

This is played each January at Melbourne Park, Melbourne, Victoria, over 14 consecutive playing days. There are day and night sessions over the first six days, and from the eighth to tenth days.

French Open

The tournament begins on the last Monday of May and goes on for 14 consecutive playing days. It is staged at the Stade Roland Garros, Paris.

Wimbledon

This begins in late June and continues until the first Sunday in July. There are 13 playing days, with no play on the middle Sunday. It is held at the All England Lawn Tennis and Croquet Club, Church Road, Wimbledon, London SW19.

United States Open

This begins in late August and continues until the second Sunday in September. There are 14 playing days, with day and night sessions over the first 11 days. It is played at Flushing Meadow, New York.

RULES CLINIC

What happens if a service is made from the wrong half of the court or the wrong end?
All play resulting from service will stand, but the moment the error is spotted the correct serving point should be taken up before the next service.

If my opponent serves and then I realize it is my turn to serve, what happens?
The fault should be rectified immediately, but all points scored before the error was noticed will count. However, if the error is noted after your opponent has served a fault, the fault does not carry over to you when you become the server.

During an indoor game, the ball from a service hits a rafter and then bounces into the correct service court. Is the service good or not?
It would be a fault. Any ball that hits a permanent fixture from the service is a fault. Permanent fixtures include such things as stands, permanent seating and their occupants . . . which could well be a judge!

If the server throws up the ball and then fails to hit it, is it a fault?
Yes. Just as in golf, it is a 'fresh air' shot, and counts.

. . . but if the server decides to abort the serve after throwing the ball up, is it still a fault?
No.

Is a let called if the ball hits the top of the net and goes into the correct court during a normal rally?
No. It can only be called a let at the service.

Can I catch the ball on my racket?
Yes, you most probably can. But if you do, the point goes to your opponent!

If I hit my racket on the ground in anger or frustration, and distort the shape of it, will I be penalized?

You are not allowed to deliberately and materially change the shape of your racket during the playing of a point. However, if you have time to damage your racket, and *then* play a winning shot you must be some player!

If I play a shot that hits the ground within the confines of the court and then hits the stop-netting at the back of the court before my opponent can reach it, is it a winning point?

Yes. The same applies if the ball hits any other permanent fixtures, provided you hit a good ball into the opposing court first.

If I return a ball and it hits the net post and then goes into the opposing court, does it count or is a let called?

It counts as a legitimate point.

What happens if my racket accidentally slips out of my hand and hits the net – do I lose the point?

Yes, provided the ball is in play at the time.

Do I have to be standing in the court to make a shot?

No. You can be anywhere, except in your opponent's area of the court.

If I play a volley close to the net, hit the ball in my half of the court, but then allow my racket to follow-through and go over the net, am I penalized?

No, but again you must make sure you don't touch the net.

Does a ball that hits another ball lying on the court have to be played as a let?

No, the shot counts.

If I am hindered from playing my shot is a let called?

Yes, unless you are hindered by a permanent fixture. If, for example, a pigeon flies across your sight just as you're about to play, that is certainly outside interference, and a pigeon could not be described as a permanent fixture.

Can the server's feet be off the ground at the time of service?

Yes, but at the moment of striking the ball his or her foot (or feet) must not touch the baseline or court the other side of the baseline.

Where does the receiver have to stand when taking the service?

Anywhere, provided it is in his or her own half of the court. Understandably, it makes sense to stand in the half of the court to where the server is serving, otherwise the job of returning the ball is considerably harder. How close you stand to the net depends on the strength of your opponent's serve.

What happens if it starts to rain while a match is in progress? Who decides when to stop and when to restart the match?

The chair umpire decides when play should halt and when the court is ready for play to resume. The tournament referee may also make the same decisions.

At what point is a match stopped because of bad light? Are there any rules relating to what constitutes bad light?

A match is, ideally, halted for bad light conditions when the games in a set are even. There are no rules relating to what constitutes bad light.

What happens if a ball hits beams or lights while in play in an indoor tournament?

The ball is out.

If the sun is strong and makes play difficult, can a player request that play be suspended until conditions improve?

A player cannot make the request. In certain climatic conditions and latitudes, where intense heat and humidity are combined, the umpire may decide to suspend play.

If my opponent is wearing reflective sunglasses that distract me, can I request that he or she removes them?

Yes. But it would require some extremely careful planning and positioning for a player wearing reflective sunglasses to be placed so that he or she created a prolonged distraction.

What happens if the ball bursts during play?

If the ball bursts, replay the point. If the ball is soft, the point stands.

What happens if the string of a player's racket or the racket itself breaks during play?

If the string breaks during the first service section, it is a fault. If the receiver's string breaks during the second service, the server reverts to a first service.

If the net falls down or breaks in some way while a point is being played, is the point replayed?

Yes. A let is called, the net is repaired, and play resumes.

Can a tie-break or final set go on indefinitely?

Yes.

If the court becomes waterlogged, muddy or damaged in any way, is play allowed to continue? At what point is play suspended due to poor conditions?

Play would not be allowed to continue. Play can be suspended on appeal from the players or, more usually, by direct action by the umpire or referee.

RANKINGS

Players on both the men's and women's tours are given individual rankings depending on the points they have earned. The higher the ranking, the more likely it is that a player will be able to enter a tournament without having to play through the qualifying rounds.

Ranking points can be earned at all levels of the game, from small satellite events to Grand Slam championships, and these are allocated according to matches won. A player who wins a match in a satellite event would gain a world ranking somewhere below the 1000 mark. There are bonus points for beating higher-ranked players.

The higher up the scale a player climbs, the greater the rewards in terms of points and of prize money. Consistent winners command the highest rankings for months and even years on end. Ivan Lendl was World No. 1 for 157 consecutive weeks and for a total of 270 weeks throughout his career. Jimmy Connors held on to the World No. 1 spot for 160 consecutive weeks and 268 weeks in all. Steffi Graf is the most dominating player of both sexes, having been World No. 1 for 186 weeks in a row. As tournaments conclude, new ranking lists are issued to reflect the previous week's activity (or two weeks' activity in the case of Grand Slam events).

The rewards at the top are considerable. By the end of 1995, Pete Sampras had won more money from the game – $21,859,428 – than any other male player. Martina Navratilova led the women's prize money list with a similarly impressive figure of over $20,000,000.

It is a long and arduous road from starting to play tennis to becoming a champion, and that route is controlled by rankings. In the UK, rankings start at competition beginner level and then progress upwards to national ranking status. As an adult player you can only obtain a world ranking by playing on the men's or women's professional

Previous pages   Every player aspires to enter Wimbledon and this panoramic view from above Wimbledon can only serve to increase the motivation of would-be champions.

Right   Steffi Graf beats Monica Seles to win the Women's Singles Final at Wimbledon in 1992.

tours. The International Tennis Federation also has world rankings for junior players. The spread of short tennis (played with softer balls and smaller-sized rackets on smaller courts) and grass-roots coaching courses means that more young children are being introduced to the game. The Lawn Tennis Association wants to encourage these young players to move on in the game and has set up starter competitions for players aged 8–18, who have won one round in any good junior tournament and live locally. The emphasis of these mainly one-day events is on enjoyment and activity.

Any match between two players who belong to the LTA-registered membership scheme will count towards a player's national rating. More information is available on this scheme (and on the LTA's events and tournaments) from its competitions and ratings department.

USEFUL ADDRESSES

National tennis associations

Argentinian Tennis Association
    Avda San Juan 1307
    1148 Buenos Aires
    Argentina

French Tennis Federation
    Stade Roland Garros
    2 Avenue Gordon Bennett
    75016 Paris
    France

German Tennis Federation
    Hallerstrasse 89
    20149 Hamburg
    Germany

Italian Tennis Federation
    Viale Tiziano
    00196 Rome
    Italy

Lawn Tennis Association
    The Queen's Club
    Barons Court
    West Kensington
    London W14 9EG
    Tel: 0171 381 7000

New Zealand Tennis Inc.
    P.O. Box 11–541
    Manners Street
    Wellington
    New Zealand

Scottish Lawn Tennis Association
    12 Melville Crescent
    Edinburgh EH3 7LU
    Tel: 0131 225 1284

Spanish Tennis Federation
    Avda Diagonal 618 3 D
    08021 Barcelona
    Spain

The Swedish Tennis Association
    P.O. Box 27915
    S–115 94 Stockholm
    Sweden

Tennis Association of the People's
    Republic of China
    9 Tiyuguan Road
    Beijing 100061
    China

Tennis Australia
  Private Bag 6060
  Richmond South 3121
  Melbourne, Victoria
  Australia

Tennis Ireland
  Argyle Square
  Donnybrook
  Dublin 4
  Ireland

Tennis South Africa
  P.O. Box 7135
  Hennopsneer
  Centurian 0046
  South Africa

United States Tennis Association
  70 West Red Oak Lane
  White Plains
  NY 10604
  USA

Welsh Lawn Tennis Association
  Plymouth Chambers
  3 Westgate Street
  Cardiff CF1 1JF
  Tel: 01222 371838

Other useful addresses

British Tennis Umpires Association,
  c/o Lawn Tennis Association
  The Queen's Club
  Barons Court
  West Kensington
  London W14 9EG

The International Tennis Federation
  Palliser Road
  Barons Court
  West Kensington
  London W14 9EG
  Tel: 0171 381 8060

INDEX

Page numbers in **bold** refer to the illustrations

artificial surfaces 13
Asociation of Tennis Professionals 49
Australian Open 51, **50**

bad light 54
balls 19–21, **21**
   faults 28–30, **30**
   'let' 28, 32, 52, 53
   out 31, **32**
   service 24–8, **26**, 52
   umpires 41
baselines 14, 16
Becker, Boris **35**
behaviour 45–8
bench press exercises **22**
'byes' 50

Capriati, Jennifer **47**
caps **10**, 11
changing ends 31, 33
clay courts 13
clothing 8–11, 45
   changing 34, **35**
club rules 45
coaches **47**, 48
code of conduct 45
Connors, Jimmy 55
continuous play 33–4
'cotton picker' exercise **23**
Courier, Jim **10**, **29**
courts 12–17

changing ends 31, 33
doubles 39, **40**
layout 13–17, **16**
surfaces 12–13
Curren, Kevin **46**

Davis Cup 50
deuce 36
double faults 28
doubles **40**
   scoring 39–40
   tournaments 49

equipment 18–21

faults
   double faults 28
   doubles 40
   footfaults **25**, 28, 53
   leaving court 47
   service 25, 52
Federation Cup 50
footfaults **25**, 28, 53
French Open 51

games, scoring 36
Graf, Steffi 55, **58**
Grand Slam championships 51, 55
graphite rackets 18
grass courts 12–13, **14–15**

handles, rackets 18

headbands **8**, 9
hindrance 31–2

indoor courts 13, 52, 54
injuries 23, 33–4
International Tennis Federation (ITF) 49, 58

knocking up 22–3

Lawn Tennis Association (LTA) 49, 58
Lendl, Ivan 55
'let' **17**, 28, 32, 52, 53
line judges 42–4, **42**
lines 14, 16

McEnroe, John **46**
Martinez, Conchita **33**
Mills, Alan **44**

Navratilova, Martina 55
net, faults 28
net-cord judges **17**, 42
nets 13–14, **16**, 54

officials 41–4

penalty points 45
permanent fixtures 17, 53
players, ranking 55–8
points
    debatable 31
    penalty points 45
    scoring 36
    winning and losing 28–31, **30**
rackets 18–19, **19**, **20**, 54
    debatable points 31
    faults 28, 53
    service 24–8, **26–7**
rain 54
rallies 28
rankings 55–8
referees, tournament 44, **44**, 50
rest periods 34, 48
Riessen, Marty **47**

Sampras, Pete 55
scoreboards **37**

scorecards 50
scoring 36–40
'seeded' players 49–50
Seles, Monica **58**
service 24–8, **26–7**
    doubles 39
    faults 25, **25**, 28, 52, 53
    'let' 28, 52, 53
service court 16–17
service line 16
sets, scoring 37
shoes 8–9, **9**, 34, 45
short tennis 58
sidelines 14
'singles sticks' 14, **16**
squat press movements **23**
Stich, Michael **44**
stretching exercises 22, **23**
strings, rackets 19, 54
sunglasses 8, 54
surfaces 12–13
suspension of play 23, 42, 54
sweet spot, rackets 18

team events 50–1
tie-breaks 36, 37, 38, 39, 54
toilet breaks 34
toss 24, **24**, 41
tournaments 49–51
    ranking lists 55
    referees 44, **44**, 50
tramlines 13

umpires 41–4, **43**, 47, 48
United States Open 51

vibration dampeners 19
volleys 53

Wade, Virginia **20**
warming up 22–3
Wimbledon **14–15**, 51, **56–8**
Women's Tennis Association 49